Blockchain Buy-In

Investing in Decentralized Assets, Startups, and Organizations

Table of Contents

Chapter 1. Introduction

Welcome to our comprehensive Special Report, "Blockchain Buy-In: Investing in Decentralized Assets, Startups, and Organizations." In a world increasingly leaning towards decentralized networks, it is important to understand and maximize the investment potential these new technological wave offers. This report simplifies the often complex labyrinth of cryptocurrencies, decentralized autonomous organizations, and blockchain-based startups. Though it may initially seem intimidating, we've boiled down the technical jargon into easily understood concepts. Enlighten yourself about this digital evolution and its financial prospects, regardless of your technical background. Empower yourself with knowledge of these new investment horizons as we reveal exciting opportunities. If you're eager to navigate the blockchain investment space, this report is just for you! There's never been a more important time to tune into the discourse of digital assets. This report is an educator, a compass, and a cheerleader, eagerly guiding you on your journey into the future of investment. So let us be your guide to the blockchain revolution - it's easier than you think!

Chapter 2. Understanding Blockchain Technology and Decentralization

The allure of blockchain technology revolves predominantly around its core principle of decentralization. Unshackling the data constraints of central systems, blockchain absolves the need for intermediaries in digital interactions, paving the way for a more autonomous, secure, and transparent network. However, the decentralized nature of blockchain that empowers this evolution often becomes a hurdle in its understanding. Even though this technology has been afloat for over a decade now, it still remains widely misunderstood. Let's start peeling off these layers of unfamiliarity and address all your blockchain queries.

2.1. Decoding Blockchain: A Brief

If you peel away all the complex terms surrounding it, blockchain can be fundamentally understood as a type of database, but with a twist. Rather than storing information in a systematic set of tables like a traditional database, a blockchain organizes data into blocks, and chains them together in an irreversible sequence.

Instead of a central authority overseeing transactions, users across the network validate and manage them. Each block contains a number of transactions, and every time a new transaction occurs on the blockchain, a record of that transaction is added to every participant's ledger, creating an encrypted, immutable, and shareable record of all transactions across the network.

Now, let's delve deeper into each of these components and their attributes.

2.2. Immutable: The Pillar of Trust

The immutability of blockchain is massively responsible for its appeal as an incorruptible digital ledger. Once a transaction is added to a block, and subsequently, the block is added to the chain, the data becomes etched into the digital stone of the blockchain record. It would need computational resources more powerful than the entire network combined to go back and alter the transaction data.

Such immutability grants transparency to the stakeholders and provides collective security against frauds – a quality dearly sought after in many use-cases like finance, real-estate, supply chain, and more.

2.3. Decentralized: The Power Distribution

Decentralization, the soul of blockchain technology, obviates the need for a central authority. Instead of information or transactions being in the hands of a single entity such as a bank or a government, it's spread across a network of peers or 'nodes.' Every node has an equal say in the validation and record of transactions.

Blockchain's decentralization fundamentally questions traditional power hierarchies and operates on a democratic, participatory approach towards data management. This form of data democracy paves the way for Decentralized Autonomous Organizations (DAOs), enabling an entirely novel way of running organizations.

2.4. Transparent: The Beacon of Accountability

Every transaction recorded on a blockchain is visible to all participants of the network, promoting transparency, and accountability. Nonetheless, it isn't an open book for everyone to pry into – the identities of the participants are cryptographically secured, usually visible as random strings of characters.

Such transparency in transactions can bring about a sea change in sectors prone to corruption or fraud, as it makes it tremendously challenging to 'cook the books.'

2.5. Secure: The Shield of Cryptography

Each step in a blockchain– from transaction validation to block formation, or block addition to the chain– is protected by cryptographic protocols. They ensure that only legitimate transactions are added and only participate with the corresponding private-key can sign off transactions.

Cryptography in a blockchain enables secure digital relationships that were impossible in the network models of yesteryears.

2.6. Anatomy of a Blockchain Transaction

Now that we've understood key blockchain attributes let's trace the journey of a transaction in a blockchain network:

1. Transaction Initiation: A participant generates a transaction using their private key.

2. Verification: The nodes in the network validate the transaction based on preset algorithms.

3. Block Formation: Once verified, the transaction is packaged with other verified transactions into a block.

4. Block Addition: The block is added to the existing chain of blocks, secured by cryptography.

5. Broadcast: The updated blockchain is broadcasted to all nodes in the network.

Now, you might be wondering, how can one build such a network? Let's answer this with understanding blockchain types and its use-cases.

2.7. Types of Blockchain and Its Use-Cases

Blockchains come in three primary forms: Public, Private, and Consortium. A public blockchain is entirely decentralized. The most well-known example of this is Bitcoin. It's open for anyone to join, validate and maintain transactions.

Private blockchains, on the other hand, limit the participation and often centralize the network to an extent – however, they do maintain the essential blockchain attributes.

Consortium blockchains are semi-private and allow only a handful of nodes to validate transactions. They're often used for inter-business dealings where only specific parties need access to the blockchain.

Whether it is enabling a decentralized digital currency like Bitcoin, recording land registries, tracking the provenance of goods, or managing a supply chain, blockchain technology holds the potential to revolutionize many areas of our digital lives.

Through demystifying the complexities around blockchain, we hope we have achieved a basic yet comprehensive understanding of the technology. This knowledge will aid in exploring the investment potentials in blockchain-centric projects or cryptocurrencies and encourage a healthy curiosity about the ongoing technological innovations around us.

In the subsequent chapters, we will explore how to leverage this technology, spot opportunities in the blockchain space, and walk you through potential investment ventures. As we unfold these insights, remember, blockchain is not just a technological change – it's a paradigm shift in how we think about authority, trust, and power in digital relationships.

Chapter 3. Demystifying Cryptocurrencies: From Bitcoin to Altcoins

In order to demystify cryptocurrencies, we must first nail down the fundamental principles that power these digital resources. At its core, a cryptocurrency is a type of digital or virtual currency that utilizes cryptography for security purposes. It operates independently of a central bank and is managed via a decentralized system, the blockchain.

3.1. A Brief History of Bitcoin: The Genesis of Cryptocurrencies

On October 31, 2008, an anonymous entity known as Satoshi Nakamoto published the Bitcoin whitepaper, setting the blueprint for the inception of Bitcoin and the entire field of cryptocurrency. Nakamoto's seminal concept combined established concepts of cryptography and digital signatures with a decentralized network of participants known as miners, who validate and confirm transactions across the system. This marked the birth of Bitcoin, the first-ever cryptocurrency.

Bitcoin was crafted in response to the 2008 financial crisis, explicitly designed to circumvent intermediary institutions (like banks) and maintain a decentralized, peer-to-peer transaction system. In essence, it was a rebellion against the traditional financial model.

3.2. Understanding Bitcoin: How It Works

Bitcoin operates on a technology called blockchain. Each block in the chain contains a list of transactions. As transactions occur, they are added to the new block to be formed. Once the block is filled up with transactions, it is added to the existing chain of blocks, thus forming a blockchain.

To ensure trust and consensus on the validity of transactions, Bitcoin deploys a mechanism known as Proof-of-Work (PoW) where miners compete to solve complex mathematical problems. The first miner to solve the problem reviews and confirms the waiting transactions and adds them to the blockchain. This process not only ensures the transparency and irreversibility of transactions but also generates new bitcoins, rewarding the successful miner with BTC.

3.3. Diving into Altcoins: Beyond Bitcoin

While Bitcoin takes the limelight as the first and the most high-profile cryptocurrency, it's just the tip of the iceberg. Since its inception, there have been thousands of cryptocurrencies created, commonly referred to as Altcoins (alternative coins).

Altcoins are stemmed from the same basic framework as Bitcoin, but developers alter the underlying coding rules to cater to a range of different functions and applications. Some aim to improve transaction speed, privacy, or the consensus mechanisms; others target entirely different spaces like smart contracts, data storage, or real-time asset trading.

3.3.1. Ethereum: a Smart Contract Pioneer

Ethereum is the second-largest cryptocurrency by market cap yet distinctively different from Bitcoin. It was proposed in late 2013 by programmer Vitalik Buterin. Ethereum operates not just as a digital currency but also as a platform that enables Smart Contracts and Distributed Applications (DApps) to be built on its platform without downtime, fraud, control, or interference from a third party.

This open access to developers who seek to write decentralized apps led to the proliferation of Initial Coin Offerings (ICOs), where startups would issue their token in exchange for 'ether' - Ethereum's native token.

3.3.2. Ripple (XRP): Banking on the Blockchain

Ripple Labs introduced XRP as a digital asset and technology protocol for facilitating real-time, cross-border payments for financial institutions. It acts as both a cryptocurrency and a technology protocol for payment networks. Its distinguishing feature is its association with the conventional banking and financial institutions, signaling the increasing acceptance of crypto-space by the traditional financial arena.

3.3.3. Litecoin: The Silver to Bitcoin's Gold

Litcoin, created by Charlie Lee, a former Google engineer, in 2011, is often considered the silver to Bitcoin's gold. It offers faster transaction confirmation times and a different hashing algorithm. Though it operates on a similar blockchain protocol as Bitcoin, it's aimed at miners who cannot afford expensive, specialized machine components to mine Bitcoin.

3.4. Navigating Cryptocurrency Investments: Risks and Opportunities

Investing in cryptocurrencies brings its share of opportunities, but it is crucial to acknowledge the accompanying risks. The immense volatility of the crypto market means that prices can skyrocket and plummet in a matter of minutes. Additionally, the lack of regulations, potential tech failures, scalability issues, and the risk of hackings & frauds make it a high-risk investment.

However, as daunting as these risks can be, there's potential for astronomical returns. Early Bitcoin investors who held onto their bitcoins have realized returns in the thousands of percent. Moreover, the increasing adoption of blockchain technology and rising acceptance of cryptocurrencies suggest a bright future for this new form of digital asset.

It's essential for anyone getting into the crypto world to conduct thorough research and consider consulting with a financial advisor. Look at market cap, trading volume, historical performance, and use cases. Read whitepapers and join online communities to learn more about the technology behind each coin before investing.

While cryptocurrencies offer a novel way to conduct transactions over the internet, investing wisely necessitates a deep understanding, cautious decision-making, and an appetite for potential risk. As we continue to explore the potential impact of the digital transformation within our global financial system, it creates a fertile ground with unlimited possibilities.

The future of cryptocurrencies may not be entirely certain but one thing's for sure - they aren't going anywhere anytime soon. As disruptive technology continues to evolve, the prospect of a decentralized financial future seems increasingly likely, marking cryptocurrencies as an asset class with great potential.

Chapter 4. The Rise and Implications of Decentralized Finance

Decentralized finance, or DeFi, is a term that has rapidly gained relevance in the world of finance and investment. It refers to the use of blockchain technologies and cryptocurrencies to recreate and improve existing financial systems. DeFi has the potential to democratize finance, rendering traditional intermediaries obsolete and enabling individuals to securely interact in a peer-to-peer manner.

4.1. The Emergence of DeFi

Decentralized finance emerged from the revolutionary technology of blockchain, the underlying tech behind digital currencies like Bitcoin. However, with the advent of Ethereum and the creation of smart contracts, the potential scope and application of blockchain technology expanded exponentially. Unlike the primarily transactional Bitcoin, Ethereum introduced programmable transactions, facilitating the rise of DeFi.

DeFi leverages smart contracts to build decentralized applications (DApps) for financial services like borrowing, lending, and investing. This development marked a shift from a digitally-transferred but ultimately centralized financial system to a truly decentralized ecosystem that eliminates intermediaries and reduces costs.

4.2. The Principles of DeFi

The DeFi movement revolves around several core principles:

1. Interoperability and Composability: DeFi applications are built on public blockchains and follow standard protocols, which allow them to complement and interact with each other. This creates an integrated financial ecosystem.

2. Permissionless and Transparent: Given the public nature of the blockchain, anyone, anywhere can access DeFi applications without needing to provide identification or other credentials. In addition, every transaction on the blockchain is publicly visible, increasing transparency and accountability.

3. Flexibility: DeFi solutions aren't just for specialists. Whether you're an average investor or a multinational corporation, the flexible nature of DeFi caters to everyone and enables a wide range of financial activities.

4.3. The Mechanism of DeFi Applications

One of the key elements driving the growth of DeFi is the emergence of decentralized applications or DApps. These are open-source applications built specifically for financial functions like lending, borrowing, and earning interest.

These applications, built on blockchain, enable users to take or give loans directly, bypassing intermediaries. They utilize smart contracts, which automatically execute deeds once predefined parameters are met, as the backbone of their system. This technology not only ensures adherence to the agreement's terms but also builds trust among participants.

These DApps effectively replace the traditional role of banks. Instead of interest rates being subject to a bank's discretion, they are driven by network supply and demand dynamics.

4.4. The Impact on the Traditional Financial System

DeFi's rise marks a significant shift in our financial paradigm. With open-source protocols and decentralized applications replacing legacy systems, it could potentially redefine our understanding of money and finance.

With DeFi, access to financial services is no longer dictated by one's geographical location or social status. Anyone with internet access can participate in this decentralized economy - a factor that could drive significant financial inclusion worldwide.

However, like any disruptive technology, DeFi faces challenges and risks. Regulatory uncertainty, the volatility of digital assets, and technological bugs are among the factors that investors must consider.

4.5. The Investment Potential in DeFi

For the forward-thinking investor, DeFi represents an intriguing investment landscape replete with opportunities. The primary means of investing lies in digital assets or tokens associated with DeFi platforms. Investors can directly purchase these tokens or earn them through "yield farming," where users commit their assets to a DeFi platform to earn returns.

Recent years have witnessed significant capital inflow into DeFi projects. The total value locked (TVL) in DeFi - a measure compared to assets under management (AUM) in traditional finance - has skyrocketed from ~$700 million in January 2020 to over $60 billion as of August 2021.

Despite its accompanying risks, the potential returns from investing in DeFi can be substantial. However, it requires careful due diligence, a willingness to embrace volatility, and a deep understanding of the technology behind it.

In conclusion, DeFi is at the forefront of the blockchain revolution, promising a future where finance is more inclusive, transparent, and efficient. It represents a fundamental shift that redefines traditional financial systems, creating exciting investment opportunities while demanding investor acumen to navigate potential risks successfully. Despite uncertainties and challenges, DeFi's principle of democratizing finance positions it as an influential force in the global economic landscape.

Chapter 5. Decentralized Autonomous Organizations: Disrupting Traditional Business Structures

In an increasingly digital age, the concept of decentralization has blurred the traditional borders between sectors, industries, and countries, creating an entirely new order, driven by technology. One such fascinating and disruptive notion is that of Decentralized Autonomous Organizations (DAOs). As a relatively nascent concept, it is pushing the boundaries of what we thought possible in organizational structure, democratization, and governance.

5.1. Understanding DAOs

Simply put, DAOs are organizations encapsulated by smart contracts on a blockchain. Smart contracts are self-executing contracts with the terms of the agreement directly written into lines of code, which autonomously control and document relevant events according to its underlying rules. DAOs run on this transparent and incorruptible system, offering a fresh approach to collaboration and decision-making.

Crucially, DAOs are entirely decentralized, without a top-down hierarchical structure. Instead, they're governed by stakeholders or members who have a say in the organization's operational and strategic decisions. This novel, democratized decision-making aspect is made possible because DAOs operate on blockchain technology, which offers a transparent, secure, decentralized, and immutable public ledger where all transactions and changes are recorded.

DAOs have the potential to disrupt the traditional business models and organizational structures that we are familiar with. They herald a move towards a system in which authority, trust, and control are distributed. This move promotes equity, transparency, and collaboration.

5.2. How Do DAOs Work?

To understand how DAOs disrupt traditional business structures, we need first to grasp how they function.

1. **Creation**: A DAO starts its life as a smart contract on a blockchain platform like Ethereum. The creators define the rules of governance, voting, and the DAO's purpose in this smart contract. The initial parameters, once defined, can't be changed. Future rule changes, new initiatives, and other significant decisions are made based on consensus mechanisms that rely on the organization's stakeholders' votes.

2. **Funding**: DAOs often obtain initial funding through a token sale, lending an initial shared asset base to kickstart their objectives. This mechanism also defines the decision-making power structure within the DAO.

3. **Operation**: The DAO essentially behaves as a shared asset pool. It can be used to fund projects or initiatives that align with the DAO's purpose, as proposed and voted on by its stakeholders.

These elements together form a functional DAO that, depending on its regulatory, operational, and economic environments, may disrupt traditional business structures.

5.3. DAOs: Disrupting Traditional Business Structures

DAOs have the potential to disrupt traditional business structures in unprecedented ways. Here's an overview of how that can happen.

5.4. Decentralized Decision Making

Traditional organizations usually have centralized decision-making structures where a board or CEO makes most of the crucial decisions. DAOs, however, operate on a principle of direct democracy, where stakeholders vote on various proposals based on the number of tokens (or stake) an individual holds. This democratic form of decision-making disposes of the hierarchy found in conventional organizations, giving power back to the stakeholders themselves.

5.5. Automated Governance

With blockchain underpinning its operation, DAOs are capable of running autonomously without any intervention. This means that once the rules are implemented, they will continue to govern each transaction or update that occurs within the DAO. Changes can only be made if the majority agree to them. This mitigates the possibilities of conflicts of interest, corruption, or power abuse seen in traditional business structures, bolstering transparency and trust.

5.6. Lower Operational Costs

DAOs virtually eliminate many traditional organizational expenses and inefficiencies associated with manual operations. They render intermediaries, such as lawyers, managers, or other roles, unnecessary because the code ensures trust and enforcement. This significantly reduces overhead, streamlines processes, and increases operational efficiency.

5.7. Fluid and Open Organizational Structure

DAOs don't have a defined, rigid structure. Their flat hierarchy allows for a greater level of flexibility and adaptability. This fluid nature also lends itself to collaboration across geographical boundaries, opening the doors for global participation and diversity.

Additionally, DAOs are open and transparent. Anyone with internet access can see how decisions are made, funds are allocated, and other activities carried out, providing an unparalleled level of transparency and accountability compared to conventional businesses.

5.8. Potential Challenges and Risks of DAOs

While DAOs present a compelling alternative to traditional business structures, they also bring a set of challenges and risks.

5.9. Regulatory Uncertainty

The intersection of technology and law remains largely uncharted. Given their decentralized nature, lack of physical presence, and global participation, DAOs can potentially circumvent regulatory frameworks of any single jurisdiction. This lack of clarity may dampen enthusiasm, as potential legal ramifications and penalties can pose significant risks.

5.10. Smart Contract Vulnerability

Despite their numerous benefits, smart contracts are also a significant risk factor. If programmed incorrectly, they can contain bugs or vulnerabilities that can be exploited by malicious parties. For instance, in 2016, a DAO known as "The DAO" was exploited due to a bug in its code, which resulted in a loss of $50 million worth of Ethereum.

5.11. Immutability Paradox

Immutability can be a double-edged sword in the context of DAOs. Once the rules and protocols are set in the smart contract and implemented, they can't be changed, ensuring security, trust, and consistency. However, this also poses a challenge as it does not allow for rectification in the presence of flaws or unforeseen circumstances.

5.12. Summary and Outlook

DAOs, backed by blockchain technology, are an exciting manifestation of decentralization that carries the potential to drastically overhaul traditional business models and operational structures. As much as they open the doors to a more egalitarian way of organizing businesses, they also pose unique challenges.

While the hurdles are significant, the potential of DAOs to engender a more open, equitable, and accountable way of conducting business might well make tackling these challenges worth the effort. As we move forward, DAOs present an exciting frontier to explore, study, and understand in the realm of business and organizational structures. If navigated judiciously, the DAO model could well herald a paradigm shift in the way organizations are run and structured, pointing towards an exciting, more equal future.

Chapter 6. Investing in Blockchain Startups: A Comprehensive Guide

One of the exciting components of the blockchain revolution lies in the potential of startups. These ventures are typically on the bleeding-edge of this technology, pioneering the path forward for blockchain's utilization across numerous sectors.

6.1. Understanding Blockchain Startups

Blockchain startups represent a new type of small-business venture that leverages advances in blockchain technology to create new business models or enhance existing ones. These startups use distributed ledger technology for a variety of purposes ranging from smart contracts to healthcare records, supply chain management, and digital identity verification, among others.

Not all blockchain startups revolve around cryptocurrency, although many do involve some aspect of tokenization. The nature of these startups lends itself to transparency, security, decentralization, and trustless transactions.

Investing in a blockchain startup involves purchasing equity or tokens in the business with the expectation that the startup will grow and the investor's stake will increase in value. However, before you put your money in a startup, you must understand what you're investing in, and whether it fits your investment strategy and risk tolerance.

6.2. Evaluating Blockchain Startups

While it might seem daunting to evaluate a blockchain startup, there are several fundamental steps to take:

1. Whitepapers: Start by studying the startup's whitepaper. Not only will this give you a deep understanding of what the startup aims to achieve, but it will also demonstrate how systematically and methodically the business plans to reach its goals.

2. Team Analysis: The people behind the startup are crucial. A capable team with experience in both the technology and business side of things is key.

3. Unique Value Proposition: It's essential to identify what sets this particular blockchain startup apart from others. What problems does it solve? How does it outperform its competitors?

4. Market Potential: Another necessary evaluation is determining if there is a genuine need or desire for the product or service in the market.

5. Tokenomics: If the startup has a token model, it is essential to understand the tokenomics involved. What is the purpose of the token? How is it used, and how will its supply and demand dynamics impact its potential appreciation?

Using these criteria as a starting point offers a framework for analyzing opportunities in the blockchain startup space.

6.3. Risk Management

As with any investment, blockchain startup investments involve risk. The sector is a modern frontier, and for every success story, there are many failures. Effective risk management includes the following strategies:

1. Diversification: The age-old adage of "not putting all your eggs in

one basket" is as relevant here as it has ever been.

2. Stay Informed: this sector is rapidly evolving, and it's essential to keep learning and stay updated on industry trends.

3. Due Diligence: In-depth research can help mitigate some risks.

Remember, investing in blockchain startups should be seen as a long-term investment. The growth cycle might be extended, and it requires patience.

6.4. Legal and Regulatory Considerations

The legal and regulatory landscape for blockchain technology and related startups is evolving. Consequently, it's important to understand these constraints before deciding to invest. Regulatory attitudes differ across jurisdictions, and laws can significantly impact the future of a startup.

Even within a country, the legal status might vary for different types of blockchain participation. For example, cryptocurrency startups might face more stringent regulation than a company using blockchain for supply chain purposes. Understanding these regulatory landscapes will also help in determining the risk associated with the investment.

To make smart investment decisions in the blockchain startup space, investors should closely monitor developments in regulations and rules.

6.5. Conclusion

Investing in blockchain startups can be an exciting journey gripping with opportunities for outsized returns. However, it's critical to approach these opportunities well-informed and prepared for potential challenges. By following a solid evaluation framework, maintaining on-going education, committing to risk management, and understanding the legal and regulatory landscape, you can become a more thoughtful and successful investor in the world of blockchain startups. Welcome to an exciting new avenue, where vision meets potential. This might just be the investment frontier you've been waiting for!

Chapter 7. Anatomy of an Initial Coin Offering (ICO)

An Initial Coin Offering (ICO) is a type of fundraising mechanism that has become a popular tool for many blockchain companies. In a nutshell, it is somewhat similar to an Initial Public Offering (IPO) but with some critical differences which we will delve into this chapter. Here, you will understand the core components, the procedure, the benefits, and the potential risks associated with an ICO.

7.1. Understanding Initial Coin Offering (ICO)

An ICO is the cryptocurrency industry's equivalent to an IPO. An ICO is a mechanism by which a new project sells its underlying cryptocurrency tokens in exchange for bitcoin and ether. This event serves two key purposes: raising funding for project development and distributing tokens to participants to be used for its functionalities.

While some might compare an ICO to a crowdfunding campaign, unlike Kickstarter or Indiegogo, an ICO is not donating money to support a product, service, or a good cause. Instead, you're putting capital, usually in the form of digital currencies, into a project in its inception, expecting a return on your investment.

7.2. How ICOs Work

Typically, in an ICO, companies create a whitepaper which outlines what the project is about, what need(s) the project will fulfill upon completion, how much funding is required for the project, the type of money accepted, and how long the ICO campaign will run for.

Individuals who financially contribute to the project during the ICO will receive tokens from the company. The tokens could have a variety of uses; some companies issue tokens that can be used as a method of payment inside their ecosystem, while others offer tokens that represent shares in the company.

If the company successfully completes the project, the value of the tokens may rise significantly, resulting in a profit for the ICO participants.

However, if the fund-raising campaign does not meet its pre-set financial goal, the money is returned to the backers, and the ICO is deemed unsuccessful.

7.3. Benefits of ICOs

On the project side, ICOs offer a number of benefits. They provide quick access to capital, offer a large pool of potential investors, and allow companies to avoid regulatory compliance procedures and costs that are associated with traditional fund-raising methods.

Investors, on the other hand, are drawn to ICOs mainly because of the potential for high returns, especially if the project proves to be successful. In addition, tokens gained in an ICO may be used to purchase goods or services offered by the company, and this utility could also add value to the tokens.

7.4. Risks Associated with ICOs

While ICOs can offer potential high returns, they also carry significant risks. The main risk is that many ICOs are for projects that are still in very early development stages, and many of them will fail. In fact, a study showed that nearly half of all ICOs in 2017 failed.

Another risk is the lack of regulatory oversight, which makes it easier for fraudulent practices to occur. There have been numerous instances of fake ICOs wherein after raising funds, the developers suddenly disappear.

Finally, the heavy reliance on cryptocurrencies for ICO transactions brings its own set of risks. These digital currencies are highly volatile, and their values often fluctuate dramatically in very short periods of time, which could affect the investor's potential return on investment.

7.5. A Brief History of ICOs

Ethereum initiated one of the biggest ICOs in history in the summer of 2014. At that time, Ethereum had proposed the development of a new blockchain that would enable smart contracts. The project raised over 18.4 million dollars within 42 days!

Since then, many other projects have followed suit with their ICOs. However, the craze for ICOs hit a peak in 2017 and early 2018, when the prices of major cryptocurrencies skyrocketed. This attracted a lot of people to the sector, eager to earn quick profits, and led to the launch of thousands of ICOs, some of which turned out to be scams.

7.6. Evaluating an ICO for Investment

Before investing in an ICO, it's crucial to conduct thorough due diligence. Here's a simple checklist:

- Mission: Identify what problem the project solves and whether it has a unique selling proposition.

- Team: Research the team behind the project. Their track record, experience, and credibility can be indicative of the project's potential success.

- Tokenomics: Check the distribution of the tokens. A good rule of thumb is that the team should not hold the majority of the tokens.

- Whitepaper: Read the whitepaper. A well-written whitepaper should explain, in detail, how the ecosystem will work.

- Roadmap: Evaluate the project's development plan. A clear roadmap suggests that the team has considered the future progression of their platform.

- Community support: A project backed by an active community is generally a good sign.

Remember, the dynamic nature of the world of ICOs and the cryptocurrencies makes it impossible to predict the future with certainty. As you become more experienced in assessing ICOs, your instinct, coupled with comprehensive analysis, will offer the best guidance.

In closing, ICOs represent a new and dynamic method of fundraising that effectively address the liquidity problems of startups. However, they also come with risks due to lack of regulatory oversight, and balancing these aspects is key to effectively navigating this new frontier in the world of investments. Knowledge, due diligence, and staying informed are your best tools as you venture into the world of ICOs.

Chapter 8. The Role of Smart Contracts in Blockchain Transactions

Smart contracts serve as the backbone of blockchain transactions, providing transparency, traceability, and tamper-proofing key features of blockchain technology. Programmed as self-executing contracts with the terms of agreement directly written into code lines, these contracts are efficient and secure means to facilitate, verify, and enforce the performance of a contract.

8.1. The Mechanism of Smart Contracts

Smart contracts are digital programs stored on a blockchain that run when predetermined conditions are met. They typically use the "IF/THEN" premise. For instance, IF Party A transfers a specific amount of cryptocurrency into the contract, THEN an agreed quantity of digital tokens or goods is released to Party A's account. This automated functionality removes the need for an intermediary, thereby reducing friction in business transactions and increasing efficiency.

Under the hood, the simplicity is backed by complex cryptographic code ensuring the transactions are secure and verifiable. Once the smart contract is deployed on the blockchain, it cannot be altered, promoting trust between parties for fair transactions.

8.2. Understanding Decentralization and Automation in Smart Contracts

Decentralization - a cornerstone of blockchain technology, plays an essential role in the efficiency of smart contracts. It provides several benefits:

- Trust: Transactions aren't controlled by a central authority; they're collectively managed by multiple nodes in the blockchain. This avoids single-point failures and malicious interventions.

- Security: As transactions are recorded across network nodes and encrypted, they are highly resistant to hacking and fraud.

- Accuracy: The automation of smart contracts reduces the possibility of manual errors.

- Speed: Automation allows transactions to be completed much faster than traditional manual processes.

By combining automation with decentralized operations, smart contracts simplify and expedite transactions, while also ensuring their validity and security.

8.3. The Nexus of Smart Contracts, Tokenization, and DeFi

Smart contracts have fueled tokenization—the act of converting rights to an asset into a digital token on a blockchain—and this has amplified the potential of decentralized finance (DeFi).

Tokenization can be used to digitize various types of assets, from tangible assets like real estate or gold to intangible assets like intellectual properties. By representing these assets as tokens on a blockchain, they can be divided into smaller, more flexible quantities allowing more potential investors to partake in the investment opportunity.

DeFi, a system where financial products become available on a public decentralized blockchain network, heavily relies on smart contracts. These platforms enable transactions of tokens between parties, without intermediaries like banks or brokers. The growth of DeFi has been mostly due to this built-in automation, increasing trust, and transparency of transactions provided by smart contracts.

8.4. Legal Standing and Regulatory Hurdles

While the promise of smart contracts is immense, legal standing and regulations are a significant part of the conversation. In current legal frameworks, contracts are typically enforced by law — a feature that smart contracts do not yet fully accommodate.

While smart contracts are inherently binding protocols, their legal standing varies across jurisdictions. Regulatory bodies around the world are attempting to understand and establish a framework for smart contracts, but many hurdles remain.

Part of the challenge in regulating smart contracts is their global nature. While they offer transcending physical borders, their enforcement and regulation are bound by the geographical boundaries and legal jurisdictions of countries.

Additionally, smart contracts pose unique challenges in dispute resolution. Due to their automated and self-executing nature, handling breaches can be complex. Traditional contracts provide terms for breach scenarios, while smart contracts do not inherently offer this.

Despite these hurdles, some jurisdictions are becoming more accepting of the legitimacy of smart contracts. These developments provide hope that the solidity and implementation of these digital contracts will continue to evolve, fostering better legal recognition globally.

8.5. Smart Contracts Evolution and Future Scope

Since their inception, smart contracts have travelled a long way, finding use in various industries such as financial services, real estate, healthcare, and supply chain management. Looking ahead, the possibilities are limitless.

Interoperability or compatibility of smart contracts across different blockchain platforms and systems will be a significant milestone in their evolution. The capability can lead to mainstream adoption of blockchain technology, offering more significant value from integration across various market sectors.

Also, smart contracts could breakthrough in Industry 4.0 applications, helping create smart factories and interconnected supply chains, promoting better resource allocation and product tracking. With IoT devices transmitting data directly into smart contracts, frictionless, automated transactions based on predefined rules are possible, creating efficient, decentralized economies of scale.

In conclusion, the revolution of smart contracts is just beginning. As more industries realize their potential, and as blockchain technology matures, smart contracts will exponentially transform the way business transactions are performed in a digital era. Much like any technology, they come along with a set of challenges; however, their promise to simplify and securitize commercial transactions should not be overlooked. The journey has just begun for these digital agreements, and the future looks incredibly promising.

Chapter 9. Investment Strategies and Risk Management in the Blockchain Market

Blockchain and cryptocurrency markets have attained significant prominence in recent years, touted as a paradigm shift in the way investment and financial transactions are conducted. This chapter aims to methodically examine investment strategies and risk management tactics uniquely suitable for this burgeoning market.

9.1. Understanding Blockchain Investments

At its core, blockchain is a decentralized database system often termed as a 'distributed ledger.' It provides a transparent, immutable, and tamper-proof record of transactions across a network of computers (nodes), thus eliminating the need for central intermediaries. On the other hand, cryptocurrencies like Bitcoin are digital assets used as mediums of exchange that utilize cryptography for security, operating on top of these blockchains.

Just like traditional markets, blockchain investments can take on many forms, and they may be direct or indirect. A direct investment in the blockchain world means buying and holding cryptocurrencies, with the hope that the value will increase over time. Indirect investing can be done through equity purchases in blockchain-based startups, buying shares in blockchain-focused funds, or investing in companies that use blockchain technology in their operations.

Before jumping onto the bandwagon, it is vital to answer some questions: What is your investment goal? How much risk can you tolerate? Do you want to opt for long-term holdings or short-term trades? What's your exit strategy? Responding to these will guide your overall investment strategy.

9.2. Cryptocurrency as an Investment Vehicle

Cryptocurrencies, such as Bitcoin and Ethereum, are an integral part of the blockchain market. The reasons for their popularity as an investment vehicle are their high liquidity, around-the-clock market operation, low entry barrier, and possibility of significant returns. However, this segment of the blockchain market is highly volatile, which is why a sound investment strategy and risk management are of utmost importance.

As a part of your crypto investment strategy, assess the market thoroughly before deciding to buy any currency. Keep tabs on market trends and conduct technical analysis to make informed decisions. Diversification is crucial here, just as it is in a traditional investment portfolio. Don't put all your investments in one currency, but rather spread it across different assets to minimize risk.

Moreover, consider dollar-cost averaging (DCA), a strategy that involves buying a fixed amount of an asset at regular intervals, regardless of its price. Over the long term, this strategy can offer lower average costs per unit due to its mitigating effect on volatility.

9.3. Investing in Blockchain Startups

Investing in early-stage blockchain startups can be highly rewarding, but it also carries substantial risks. Unlike traditional businesses, the value proposition of these startups is often pegged to innovative, anticipated use cases of blockchain technology, which may or may not materialize or become financially viable.

Before investing, scrutiny of the startup's business model is necessary. Assess their product-market fit, competitive advantage, and the experience and expertise of the team behind it. Also, consider legal compliance and the startup's roadmap for future growth, including how they intend to use the funds raised.

One way to invest in startups is through Initial Coin Offerings (ICOs) or Security Token Offerings (STOs), where tokens or cryptocurrency are sold to early backers of a project. Due diligence is especially crucial here due to the many instances of fraudulent offerings in the past.

9.4. Applying Traditional Risk Management Techniques

Risk management is vital in this market, characterized by high volatility and regulatory ambiguity. Traditional risk management techniques surprisingly can be applied here, with some adaptation.

Portfolio diversification, as discussed, lessens the impact any one investment can have on your overall performance. Close attention to regulatory updates can equip for sudden market changes, as blockchain regulations are still evolving worldwide. Regular monitoring of your investments is essential due to the market's 24/7 operation, which can lead to drastic price changes over short periods.

One important piece of advice: Always invest an amount that you are willing to lose.

9.5. Leveraging Tools and Platforms for Blockchain Investments

A multitude of tools and platforms are available today, aiding your analysis and decision-making process in the blockchain market. Cryptocurrency exchanges, wallet services, blockchain explorers, and analytics tools are some categories to consider.

Choose cryptocurrency exchanges and wallet services with a reliable security record. Remember, transactions on the blockchain are irreversible. Blockchain explorers can provide useful insights about network activity, token transfers, and overall network health. Analytics tools can support in-depth market analysis by providing data on market trends, trading volumes, and social media sentiments about different blockchain assets.

9.6. Preparing for Market Volatility

Finally, being mentally prepared for market volatility can help you make thoughtful decisions rather than being driven by emotion or panic. The market can swing wildly in either direction in a matter of hours. Having a well-thought-out investment strategy, taking calculated risks, being patient, and not succumbing to the market's euphoria or pessimism is the way forward.

Entirely eliminating risk in these nascent markets may not be practical. Instead, understanding it and strategically positioning oneself to mitigate potential negative impacts would be key to carving a successful investment journey in the world of blockchain.

Chapter 10. Emerging Trends in Blockchain Technology

Revolution in technology is an integral part of the 21st century, and the recent surge of interest in decentralized networks is a testament to that. Blockchain, the underlying technology of bitcoin and several other digital assets, has shown immense potential that transcends traditional currencies and has given birth to numerous other applications.

10.1. Blockchain: A Brief Overview

Before delving into the emerging trends in blockchain technology, let's briefly touch upon what blockchain is. At its heart, the blockchain is a type of distributed ledger, an extensive database that's shared and synchronized across multiple sites, institutions, or geographies. It allows transactions, agreements, contracts, and other activities to be recorded transparently and securely, reducing the risk of fraud while improving overall efficiency.

Every new transaction that occurs is grouped with other transactions into a block. This block is then attached to the existing blockchain, forming a chain of blocks - hence "blockchain." Notably, these transactions are verified by network nodes, known as miners, through cryptography, providing a high level of security.

10.2. The Advent of Blockchain 2.0 and 3.0

Blockchain 1.0 was primarily focused on cryptocurrencies. However, over time, technologists started realizing its potential for broader use cases. This gave birth to Blockchain 2.0 and Blockchain 3.0, which encompassed smart contracts and decentralized applications (DApps), and the integration of physical systems with blockchain respectively.

Today these further evolved forms of blockchain are increasingly being used to revolutionize multiple industries, from healthcare to supply chain management, insurance, finance, and more. The emerging trends we'll discuss in this chapter draw largely on these advanced forms of blockchain technology.

10.3. Rise of Decentralized Finance (DeFi)

One of the most impactful trends to emerge in recent years is Decentralized finance (DeFi). This new financial architecture leverages key principles of the blockchain to create an open, transparent, and permissionless financial system. It enables multiple financial activities like lending, borrowing, and trading to be performed without the need for intermediaries like banks or financial institutions.

DeFi platforms also make use of programmable contracts known as smart contracts. They're self-executing contracts with the terms of an agreement directly written into code. This feature allows for the creation of more complex, trustless interactions, revolutionizing the way traditional financial transactions are conducted.

One of the significant advantages of DeFi is that it is more inclusive. Unlike traditional finance that requires users to have a bank account, DeFi platforms can be accessed by anyone with an internet connection.

10.4. Enterprise Blockchain Adoption

Many companies are beginning to understand how blockchain technology can help streamline business processes. This has led to a rise in enterprise blockchain adoption. These blockchain systems can provide businesses with enhanced security, cost-efficiencies, and improved traceability.

Industries like Supply Chain Management, Healthcare, and Insurance are finding blockchain to be beneficial. For instance, in supply chain management, the blockchain can provide end-to-end visibility of goods, right from the manufacturer to the final consumer, ensuring product authenticity and combating counterfeit goods.

10.5. Non-Fungible Tokens (NFTs)

Non-Fungible Tokens (NFTs) have gained significant traction in 2020 and 2021. Unlike cryptocurrencies like Bitcoin or Ethereum, which are fungible and can be exchanged on a one-for-one basis, NFTs are unique digital assets that cannot be replaced with something else.

NFTs are built using the same blockchain technology that powers cryptocurrencies, but they're a new type of digital asset. They're part of the Ethereum blockchain-based ERC-721 standard. This uniqueness gives them value, especially for digital art, where they can prove ownership of a digital creation.

10.6. Cross-Chain Compatibility

One of the considerable challenges in the blockchain world is the lack of interoperability between different blockchain networks. However, a growing trend is the development of techniques and technologies that allow for seamless communication and interaction between multiple blockchain networks.

Cross-chain technology could potentially revolutionize the blockchain space by enabling different blockchain networks to share information and value. It would foster a whole new level of collaboration and integration between blockchain networks, creating a unified and far more powerful blockchain ecosystem.

10.7. The Quantum Threat and Post-Quantum Cryptography

Quantum computing is an emerging field of technology that could potentially disrupt many of our current technological realities, including blockchain. The power of quantum computers threatens the cryptographic processes upon which blockchain security depends.

However, as quantum computers become more powerful, blockchain professionals and cryptographers are working on cryptographic algorithms that can withstand quantum attacks. This concept, known as post-quantum cryptography, has been gaining attention in the blockchain world and can potentially future-proof blockchain technology.

Blockchain technology has grown beyond its initial purpose of supporting cryptocurrencies. Today, it holds the potential to transform industries, power new business models, and democratize access to services worldwide. As the technology continues to evolve, it's bound to raise new discussions, introduce new concepts, and reveal new investment opportunities. Navigating this landscape may seem daunting, but equipped with a fundamental understanding of blockchain technology, an investor can make informed and compelling decisions about where to place their bets in this evolving market.

Chapter 11. The Future of Investing in Blockchain: Opportunities and Challenges

As we proceed further into the 21st century, the blockchain revolution continues to offer a wealth of untapped potential. With unique opportunities also come unique challenges, especially in terms of investment. Dive deep into the future of blockchain investment, its potential pitfalls, and how successful investors will acclimatize.

11.1. The Investment Landscape Transformed by Blockchain

Blockchain does to asset management what the internet did to information. It has ushered in an era of decentralization, transparency, and efficiency with potential to revolutionize many sectors. Especially finance.

Traditional investments typically involve a centralized authority or third-party that ensure transactions take place without any foul play. Not only does blockchain technology eliminates the need for a central authority, it achieves this in a transparent and tamper-evident manner.

Blockchain investments are not restricted to digital currencies. From equity tokens (ownership in a company) to non-fungible tokens (NFTs — unique digital certificates supporting assets), blockchain unlocks a vast universe of unqueried investment opportunities.

11.2. Decentralized Finance (DeFi) and Smart Contracts

In the vanguard of blockchain's financial revolution is Decentralized Finance or DeFi. DeFi represents the move from a centralised financial system towards an ecosystem without intermediaries such as banks, brokers, or exchanges. All transactions are managed by smart contracts on blockchain, further magnifying transparency.

Smart contracts are programmed to automatically enforce themselves once certain pre-set conditions are met. This can reduce fraud and increase simplicity, efficiency, and interoperability.

Being on the blockchain, DeFi investments offer accessibility, inclusivity and reward potential. Investors worldwide can access various products like borrowing, lending, insurance, and yield farming, previously only available to institution-affiliated individuals.

11.3. Tokenization and Real-world Asset Interfacing

Blockchain's tokenization feature can interlink the digital and the physical worlds. Tokenization refers to the conversion of real-world assets like real estate, equity, and artwork into digital tokens, facilitating fractional ownership, ease of trade, and increased liquidity.

Blockchain assets are serialized, creating an immutable and reliable record of the asset's entire lifecycle. This, in turn, can provide certainty to investors about the authenticity and the value of their investments.

11.4. Opportunities in the Blockchain Space

Undeniably, blockchain creates a treasure trove of investment opportunities. Apart from cryptocurrency, blockchain securities, tokenized goods, and DeFi offerings, blockchain can also offer space for investing in infrastructure, platforms, and services providing the backbone of this emerging ecosystem.

But one should remain vigilant due to unchartered waters filled with regulatory uncertainties, vulnerabilities, and market volatilities.

11.5. Confronting Challenges: Regulatory Uncertainty

Blockchain technology and digital assets represent an unfamiliar territory for policymakers around the world, leading to regulatory uncertainty.

Different countries approach it differently, from open support, careful neutrality, to outright bans. This patchwork approach by regulators may lead to jurisdictional discordance, affecting the stability and confidence of investors.

11.6. Problems of Security

While blockchain's decentralized nature is a strength, it poses novel security challenges. The manipulation by bad actors may lead to substantial losses. Smart contracts, though revolutionary, are as secure as they are coded to be. Bugs and errors can lead to devastating results.

Further, the lack of recourse in the digital asset space means investments are not FDIC insured like with traditional banking systems. If a blockchain network or wallet service gets hacked, investors may have nowhere to turn.

11.7. Market Volatility and Liquidity Risks

Investment in blockchain undergoes considerable short-term price volatility. The high-reward high-risk paradigm rings especially true in this context.

Moreover, while some blockchain investments may be highly liquid like Bitcoin or Ethereum, others may struggle with low market demand, thereby posing liquidity risks.

Being an early stage technology, investments in blockchain startups can be a high risk-reward play, requiring thorough due diligence.

11.8. Overcoming the Challenges

Educating investors about the blockchain environment, relevant risks, and mitigation strategies are essential. More nuanced and articulated regulation, globally harmonized, can provide necessary legitimacy and trust.

Security measures and best practices like regular software updates, multi-factor authentication, hardware wallets, and insurance can prevent unauthorized access and reduce risk.

Finally, a more sophisticated understanding of this market's volatility, diversification of portfolio, and disciplined investing are key in managing the challenges of market volatility and liquidity risk.

Blockchains' potential to instigate change is unignorable. While challenges persist, the myriad opportunities and potential returns make the prospect of investing in blockchain an exciting proposition.

With the right knowledge, tools, and a measured approach, one might navigate these promising yet turbulent waters.

As we journey through this era of digital revolution, it is crucial to learn, adapt, and invest wisely. After all, the future is unfolding right before us. In blockchain, we trust.